I0019534

Just Enough Debugging

Debugging, Refactoring, and Unit Tests

1st Edition

Just Enough Debugging

Debugging, Refactoring, and Unit Tests.

An Introduction to debugging code, refactoring it to be efficient, readable, and extensible, and ensuring it stays functional using unit tests.

Part of the "Just Enough" series on the practices and techniques of software development.

Ed Crookshanks
Nokel Services
Spring 2018

Cover image: Kelsey Crookshanks

ISBN-13: 978-1985261815
ISBN-10: 1985261812

Version 2018-Spring

To Amy, Noah, and Kelsey

Table of Contents

Preface

About the "Just Enough" Series

This series of books is aimed at programmers who are new to formal development, or those seasoned programmers who would like to gain an understanding of processes they haven't used or been exposed to. Common examples would be recent graduates or those taking some type of "Software Practicum" course; someone who is self-taught or a hobbyist and is looking to move to the corporate world; or someone who has worked in very small software organizations where development is less controlled. Although there may be statements about retail software the emphasis is mainly on enterprise software within a medium to large organization.

Each book provides a relatively brief but in-depth discussion of its topic. While I dare not say that each book "is really all you need to know" on a particular topic, I feel that the major points and most frequently used practices and techniques are discussed. There are thousands of software producing organizations out there and there is no way to even come close to discussing the fine points that each organization uses. However there are some common practices and techniques that are the same or similar in principle. My aim is to keep these topics relatively short and more at a "getting started" level than a "deep dive" into each. As someone who has interviewed many people I can attest to the fact that hearing "I'm familiar with the concept and I've worked through some examples" is much better than "I've never heard of or used that technique." At the very least during interviews I hope to enable the first answer with books in this series.

Another reason that I'm not going into extreme detail on each topic is that there are many other books with hundreds of pages that do that. I would rather introduce these topics to a level that is quickly usable, thereby letting the reader decide which to investigate further based on experience or interest. Learning, especially in IT/programming, is a life-long pursuit and while techniques usually change slower than technology both do evolve at a pace that is quicker than other engineering disciplines.

With that, I hope to keep each book in this series at under one hundred pages and group the topics so that they flow together and are complementary. Brevity will be key in that; examples will be kept simple and code will often be "snipped" to exclude items not directly being discussed.

Notes about Software

Examples are provided mostly in C# and different tools, all of which have some level of free software available, such as Visual Studio Community Edition. Enterprise versions of these tools may exist, or similar tools with stricter licensing models and slightly different semantics may exist; it is simply assumed that tools at the educational level will be closer to the free versions. Also, most hobby developers or recent graduates will probably make use of free tools instead of starting with an expensive development tool suite. If a particular topic/example is not given in a familiar language or with a familiar tool it should be easily translated into another environment. Where possible, notes on how different platforms solve different problems in different ways will be noted. Some of these tools may already be mandated by an employer, others may be free to choose which tools to use to start a practice discussed here.

Please note – the examples will be kept necessarily simple. In fact, most of the examples will be so short that the tools and techniques used on them will probably not seem worth it. However in the context of much larger systems, enterprise systems, these tools and techniques are very useful.

Author Summary
Ed Crookshanks has over 20 years of experience in software development.   He started with C on a VAX machine for medical research, moved on to C++ on both Unix and PC platforms, database programming, and finally added some Java and .NET in a wide variety of business domains.   He is also a former adjunct professor and a Microsoft Certified Trainer delivering classes on SQL Server and Visual Studio.   A full bio can be found at http://www.nokelservices.com/bio.html.

Introduction

Debugging is a very important but often overlooked activity in software development. It is crucial to helping a developer understand what is happening when code is not behaving correctly. While many will 'pick this up' along the way there are some important techniques that every coder can use. There are also a plethora of tools available that assist the programmer in looking at code with the intention of finding and eliminating bugs. Becoming familiar with the tools and techniques in this book can potentially help the reader be more productive and find bugs quicker.

Unlike many other areas of software development, and despite what many may feel, debugging is not an entirely theoretical learning process. Experience does play a factor. Since many bugs are only evident through observed behavior (or misbehavior) having "seen that before" will often be a large help. Of course there are some bugs that could be caught in code reviews and other peer processes but these may happen much later after the code is written and first tested/observed by the coder.

There is also an ongoing discussion about what exactly constitutes a 'bug'. Is it a logic error? A system exception? Code mishandling bad input? I will not wade into that debate here; my intent is to simply show how to inspect code and remove bugs/errors no matter what they are called.

In this book I will cover several aspects of bugs – some simple definitions, techniques, tools, and strategies for employing them. I will also cover two closely related topics – unit testing and refactoring. Both of these ancillary topics could potentially have their own dedicated book but here I will discuss them in the context of supporting debugging.

Also note that debugging as discussed in this book is all about Visual Studio and .NET. However most programming environments and IDEs offer similar functionality whether visually or through another interface. For example, Java development in Eclipse® or NetBeans® offers very similar methods for breakpoints, stepping, immediate windows, etc. And similar libraries are available for unit testing and logging, some even being language ports between .NET and Java. Python offers debugging support through its IDLE IDE and although not quite as polished as the IDE-integrated tools the terms and concepts are similar.

Simply put, if Visual Studio is not your tool of choice, the concepts and terms discussed here will still apply. And it always nice to have experience and exposure to multiple tools and languages.

Debugging

Theory

As mentioned in the introduction the term 'bug' can sometimes be thought of in different ways. Some purists differentiate between a bug, an error, and an exception. Here I will use the general term "bug" and hence the process of finding and eliminating them as "debugging." Different tools can indeed help find different kinds of issues but I will stick with the high-level ones here. Also, the proliferation of more and more abstract languages has somewhat removed the need to dive deep into things like memory leaks, page faults, and buffer issues, so those will not be discussed here.

The bugs that will be examined are not necessarily the focus of this book, rather the tools and techniques used to look for and address them. There are several good books out there on writing high-quality code, defensive coding, etc. And while the nature of the bug isn't terribly important here, bugs can roughly be broken into two large groups – design bugs and coding bugs.

Design bugs can be thought of as code that does not meet the end user's expectations. In short the code may function correctly but not as expected. There can be many reasons for this, from poorly written specifications to simple misinterpretations. The important thing to note is that often these bugs will not result in a crash or otherwise easily observable problem. For example if the program outputs a file with the name "File_1.txt" and the user was expecting "File_2016_5_15.txt" that would be a design bug.

Coding bugs are issues that result directly from code. From unchecked array bounds to non-validated input to taking the length of an empty string – these may or may not result in a big crash. But they often result in strange behaviour and strange observable results. Typically these are what people think of as "bugs" although they are sometimes referred to as errors or exceptions depending on how they manifest themselves.

So given these broad types of bugs, how are they located? What tools are available and how are they used? The rest of this section demonstrates the many techniques that can be used when debugging code.

Console Output

The most basic form of finding out what is going on inside of a program is the simply print a message to the console. From the days of C this is often called `println()` or `printf()` debugging as those were the C function calls to produce the output. This type of output can often be seen when installing programs from a command line or as part of an installer.

To keep the debug statements separate from the normal console output or status updates, especially for console programs, a function can be defined that makes the debug statements stand out. The code in Listing 1 shows how a simple function can be defined that decorates debug output so it can be easily spotted in the console. Listing 2 shows how the function can be used with other output statements and Figure 1 shows this looks in the console.

```
static void Debug(String output)
{
    Console.WriteLine(" ** DEBUG: " + output);
}
```

Listing 1

```
static void GetGreeting()
{
    Console.Write("Enter your name to
                   receive a greeting: ");
    toGreet = Console.ReadLine();
    Debug("Read in: " + toGreet);
}
```

Listing 2

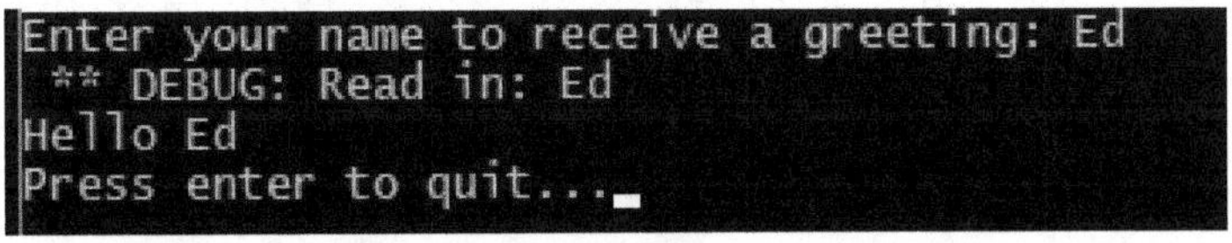

Figure 1 – Debug statements in the console

While this type of debugging can be quite useful, it does present a few challenges. One is that the statements are part of the code. Meaning that if the programmer doesn't output a certain value it won't be seen.

Also, if the program crashes in between statements the location can only be traced by what has been seen and what has not. Depending on how far apart the statements are this could be quite a lot code to examine. This also implies that the debug code also has to be maintained. When new variables, functions, or other statements are added the Debug () calls also have to be added for the new code to be inspected. Finally, the debug code is additional code that is compiled in with the executable and makes the compiled code larger.

The many drawbacks of outputting debug information to the console limit its usefulness in all but the simplest applications. Most important are the intrusive nature of the debug statements and the requirement of maintaining it. Before discussing ways of non-intrusively inspecting code the different ways to compile the code should be highlighted.

Debug vs Release

When compiling an application there are two ways to build the code – Debug mode and Release mode. As their names suggests they are optimized for different abilities. Release code is smaller, optimized for speed, and doesn't include any unnecessary overhead. This is what should be released into production or to platforms where space is a concern such as mobile devices.

Debug mode includes libraries and "hooks" into the code to allow for interactive debugging. This typically makes the code larger and relatively slower than release code. It does however allow for running inside of Visual Studio in an interactive mode which will be discussed shortly.

The Debug configuration also contains pre-defined symbols that can leveraged to "conditionally compile" code. One of the most popular is the DEBUG constant. This can be used in conjunction with a pre-processor statement to have the compiler decide whether or not to include marked code. These statements are evaluated before the code is compiled and if the value is present the code is included, otherwise it is removed. This is shown in Listing 3. The affect is to remove the output statement from release builds such that the Debug() function simply becomes an empty no-output call.

```
static void Debug(String output)
{
    #if DEBUG
    Console.WriteLine(" ** DEBUG: " + output);
    #endif
}
```

Listing 3

Debug mode should normally only be compiled and used locally due to the increased size and slower speed. However in some cases it may be deployed as long as the size and speed requirements are noted and accepted. This may aid in remote debugging which will be discussed later. The main purpose for using Debug code is to allow for inspection while running through the development environment. The following sections detail many of the tools for this, beginning with Breakpoints.

Breakpoints

Simply put, a breakpoint is a location in the source code where the execution will stop when debugging. The development environment will stop program execution at the line where the breakpoint occurs and give the developer a chance to inspect that line along with other conditions that exist at that point.

In Visual Studio a breakpoint is set but clicking in the "gutter" on the far left of the editing window. A red dot will appear and the line corresponding to the dot will have a red background. The screenshot in Figure 2 below shows a line with the breakpoint symbol to the left and the highlighted line to the right.

Figure 2 - Breakpoint

Clicking in the gutter is the quick way; this can also be done through a context menu on any line, or by placing the cursor on a line and pressing F9. The Debug menu also allows for creating a breakpoint, as well as Deleting All or Disabling All breakpoints. These two options could come in handy if there is an overwhelming number of breakpoints and removing or disabling them all at once makes the most sense.

The line of code in Figure 2 is part of bigger function. This is the function that will be the basis for many of the upcoming discussions. A picture of the code, including line numbers and without the breakpoint, is shown below in Listing 4 for reference.

```
38    public void CalculatePremium()
39    {
40        Random r = new Random();
41        double randFactor = r.NextDouble();
42
43        int topPremium = 1000;
44        int ageDiscount = (int)(Age * (randFactor/2) * 10);
45        int ticketDiscount = SpeedingTickts == true ? 0 : 200;
46
47        int yearsDiscount = (int)(YearsDriving * randFactor);
48
49        // Subtract all discounts
50        int calculated = topPremium - ageDiscount -
51                         ticketDiscount - yearsDiscount;
52
53        InsurancePremium = MinimumCheck(calculated);
54
55    }
56
```

Listing 4

In Visual Studio a program can be stared in Debug mode in several ways. One is to use the menu system and choose "Debug->Start Debugging". Another is to press the "F5" hotkey although this is configurable by both user and language preference. A very popular way is to use the Debug toolbar and press the "play" button which is often combined with the word "Start". This also has the convenience of being near the dropdown boxes for choosing the configuration and CPU targets; this can be advantageous when working with multiple configurations or targeting multiple CPUs with mobile development. That will not be embellished on here but the toolbar is shown in Figure 3.

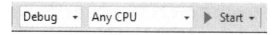

Figure 3 - Debug Toolbar

Once started in Debug mode, the application will start and run. If the program has breakpoints the code will execute until it reaches the breakpoint and then stop. The IDE should come to the front and should stop at the first Breakpoint it encountered. This is shown below in Figure 4.

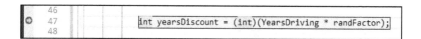

Figure 4 - Hitting a Breakpoint

Once a Breakpoint is reached there are several pieces of information available and several options for continuing. The quickest is hovering the mouse over any single piece of the expression. Doing so will create a popup showing the value of that variable. There are also many dedicated windows for debugging as well that show up only when debugging. The default configuration of windows is shown in Figure 4. Each of the tabs will be discussed before moving to some of the additional windows available and some of the actions available.

The Output window behaves similar to a console output. In the case of a GUI or web application statements written to the Console appear here. For a console application the debug statements from the framework will be seen here while the console output goes to the actual DOS console.

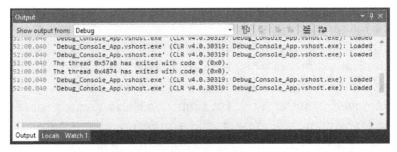

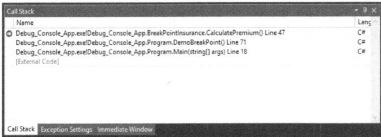

Figure 5 - Default Debug windows

Both the Locals Window and Watch Window are for observing the value of variables. However they are populated and used slightly differently.

Variables and values in the Locals Window are populated by the debugger and represent what is in the current scope. Within a method this would include all variables inside that method. If the method is part of a class (as it usually is) this would include the containing object as well since that method is part of the object and the object is accessible from within the method.

The Watch Window is user populated. Both variables and expressions with variables can be put here. They are added by many different methods. One is when at a breakpoint, right clicking on a variable and choosing "Add Watch" from the context menu. This will place the variable in the watch window for the current and subsequent runs until it is removed. Another way is to simply click on an empty space in the window and enter a valid expression. When the values are in scope they will be populated; when they are not in scope they will be dim and disabled. Figure 6 shows a screengrab of the Watch window with both a variable and two expressions; the code is stopped at the same line as in Figure 4.

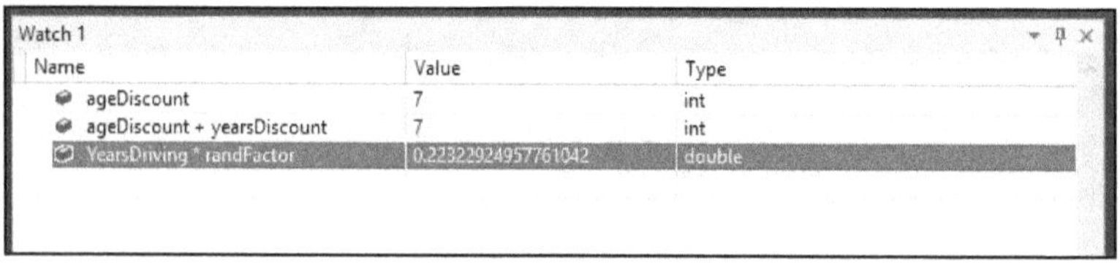

Watch 1			▾ ⊓ ×
Name	Value	Type	
● ageDiscount	7	int	
● ageDiscount + yearsDiscount	7	int	
☼ YearsDriving * randFactor	0.22322924957761042	double	

Figure 6 - Watch Window populated

The Immediate Window can also be used to observe the values of variables and calculate expressions. When at a breakpoint, typing in the name of a variable or expression preceded by a question mark (?) will display the current value. However with the Immediate Window the value of a variable can be updated in real time. This can be an immense help as the developer can literally change values to represent scenarios that the code may not be going through. Figure 7 shows the Immediate Window with both value query and an expression to update the value.

```
Immediate Window
?randFactor
0.2585924818453344
randFactor = .98022
0.98022
```

Figure 7 - Immediate Window

If the changes in the immediate window affect values in other windows, such as the Watch or Local Windows, those values will appear in red in those places to signify a change. This happens if values are updated via the Immediate Window or through the course of normal program execution. Executing the program in Debug Mode is often done through "stepping" which will be discussed next.

Stepping through code is a very common, and extremely useful, way to inspect running code. In addition to the Debug Windows mentioned previously, the menu system also changes slightly when running in Debug mode. Specifically the Debug menu becomes active and several buttons are added to the toolbar. These are shown in Figure 8; the additional buttons to the right of the search folder icon and separator are visible during debugging.

Figure 8 - Debug Menu Items

These additional button allow for control over the code when in Debug mode. The Pause button allows for pausing running code on its current statement. If there are no breakpoints in the code and the developer wants to stop and examine where the program is, pressing this button breaks at the current statement. The other two buttons in that section – the red square and the counter-clockwise circle arrow – stop the program and restart the program respectively.

The clockwise circle arrow is disabled here because the application is simple console app. For Windows Phone applications this allows for changing the UI on the fly and refreshing immediately to see the changes.

The next four buttons – the right facing arrow and the three small arrows and dots – implement the main functionality of single-step debugging. Note also that each of these buttons also have hot-keys that are different depending on the default language preferences as well as being completely configurable via custom settings. The discussion below will reference the default settings for C# development.

The first button, →, is for Show Next Statement (hot keys Alt+Num *). This is useful if stepping through code and also looking around at variables in other locations. When this is pressed the cursor will move to the next statement to be executed.

The down arrow and dot, ↓, is used to Step Into (hot key F11) a section of code. If the code is stopped and the current line contains a function or functions, pressing this will go into the first (or only) function and break at the first line in the function. From there normal stepping is available.

Note that stepping into a function may not always be possible. To step into a function the debugging code for that function must be available. Third party libraries or native Operating System calls might not have this information available. If the call cannot be accessed the debugger will simply move onto the next statement and behave like the next button – Step Over.

The semi-circle arrow around the dot, ⟳, is to Step Over (F10) the current line of code. This simply executes the current line, moves to the next executable statement, and stops before executing it. Repeatedly pressing this button will move a single line at a time through the code. This is the epitome of single stepping and is probably the most used feature in debugging. Not only are variables and expressions visible in the previously discussed windows, but often times stepping in this manner can reveal flow errors due to conditions that may be hard to see by simply watching the output.

Simply putting a breakpoint on a line that contains a variable only gives information about the code at that point. If the line was part of a larger method what happened before or after may not be immediately apparent. But by putting a breakpoint at the start of the method and stepping through every single line, the developer will get an idea of how the overall flow goes. This may reveal behaviours based on runtime information that isn't available when coding - such as how the code flows through a series of complex if statements. Doing so would reveal where and how a value was populated rather than just looking at the value at the breakpoint line.

The final circle and arrow, ⬆, is used to Step Out (Shift+F11) of a method. This is just the opposite of Step Into; Step Out runs the remaining statements of the current method and breaks at the line following the method call.

Note that although Step Over is by far the most common task it may often lead to the use of others. For example, if stepping through code and a value returned from a function is unexpected, the developer may Step Into the function the next time through. Then if in the process of stepping through that function the reason for the unexpected value is found they may Step Out and continue on. Or alter the value with the Immediate Window discussed previously before continuing.

In addition to the buttons on the default Debug Menu, other items are available while stepping through code by right-clicking and bringing up the context menu. The Debug options available are shown in Figure 9. All of them will not be discussed but the next few paragraphs will highlight a few of the most commonly used.

The Add Watch command has already been alluded to earlier in the discussion of the Watch Window. Quick Watch will bring up a pop-up window immediately and display the value of a variable or allow editing an expression. From there the window can be closed or the value added to the normal Watch Window. This is a little more effort than simply hovering over a variable to see the value but is useful for expressions.

Step Into Specific is used for stepping into a chosen function. It is more selective than the normal Step Into as it allows the developer to control which function to enter If there are more than one on the current line.

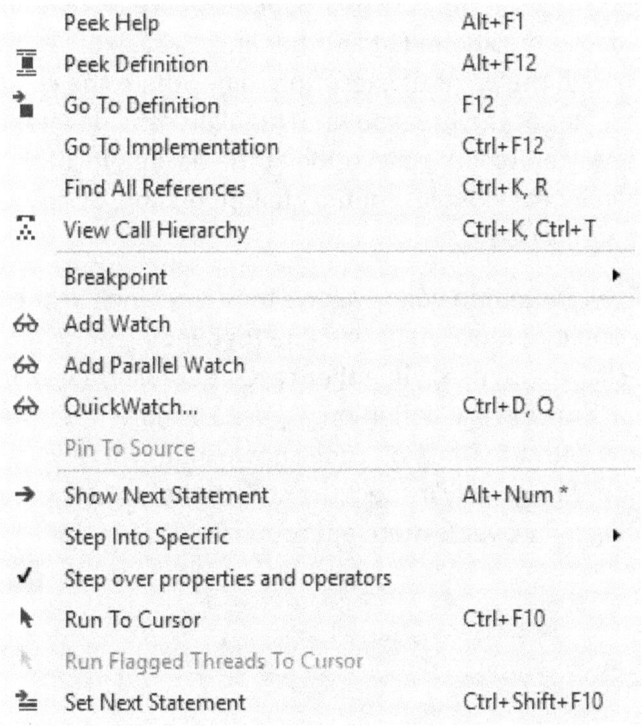

Peek Help	Alt+F1
Peek Definition	Alt+F12
Go To Definition	F12
Go To Implementation	Ctrl+F12
Find All References	Ctrl+K, R
View Call Hierarchy	Ctrl+K, Ctrl+T
Breakpoint	▶
Add Watch	
Add Parallel Watch	
QuickWatch...	Ctrl+D, Q
Pin To Source	
Show Next Statement	Alt+Num *
Step Into Specific	▶
Step over properties and operators	
Run To Cursor	Ctrl+F10
Run Flagged Threads To Cursor	
Set Next Statement	Ctrl+Shift+F10

Figure 9 - Debug Context Menu

Both Run to Cursor and Set Next Statement are very useful in controlling execution. If the cursor is at a location other than the current break statement, Run to Cursor will execute all statements between the current statement and the cursor location. This is actually a time saver as rather than single stepping through a block of statements the developer can choose to execute them without review.

Set Next Statement can be used in the opposite manner of Run to Cursor. If the code is stopped at a breakpoint and the cursor is positioned at another line, Set Next Statement will change the point of execution to be where the cursor is located, not at the breakpoint. This allows the developer to skip code and resume execution at the desired location. This can be for troubleshooting, failure testing, or any number of reasons.

The Peak Definition action allows for a brief look at the definition of a function or variable (depending on where the right-click happened). In either case a sub-window will appear showing the definition. Figure 10 shows the sub-window with the function code shown in it. This allows the developer to quickly inspect the code to help determine if stepping in or over is more appropriate.

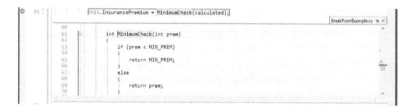

Figure 10 - Peek at Function Code

Go To Definition and Go To Implementation will actually take the developer to the each of those points in the code rather than opening a sub-window. If the function in question is in an interface, Definition is where the function is defined and Implementation is where it is actually implemented. For non-interface functions this would be the same location.

The previous sections have covered execution control via the step functionality; there is one final aspect of debug flow control. Conditional Breakpoints are just like normal Breakpoints with the exception that they are defined with a conditional statement and they only break if that statements evaluates to true.

A conditional Breakpoint is set on a line just like a normal Breakpoint – using the hot-key, menu system, or clicking on a line in the gutter. Initially this is just a normal Breakpoint. However by right-clicking and choosing "Conditions..." the sub-window shown in Figure 11 will be displayed. Also note that once a condition is set the Breakpoint icon will have a white plus in the center. This allows for easily distinguishing between normal and conditional Breakpoints.

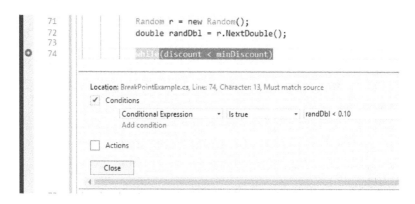

Figure 11- Conditions for a Breakpoint

The first dropdown box is for choosing the type of expression. There are three types – Conditional Expression, Hit Count, and Filter. Each can be used only once so a compound condition of three expressions is possible.

The Conditional Expression can have the evaluation of "Is True" and "When Changed". The expression in the third box is what is evaluated and can be as simple or as complex as needed. The difference is that for "Is True" the code will stop each time if the expression is true. For "When Changed" the code will only break of the expression changes between runs. The first time through is not counted as a change so that is another consideration as well.

Hit Count is another condition; this will activate the breakpoint once the Breakpoint has been hit the specified number of times. This can be equal to a specific number, greater than a specific number, or a multiple of a specific number. This can be advantageous when processing large lists of objects.

Filter is mainly used for multithreaded programming, as the filter condition is for inspecting properties of the running code such as Machine ID, Thread ID, Process ID, etc.

The Action checkbox is for adding a message to the output window and deciding whether to actually stop or not. Figure 12 shows the use of a predefined debug macro ($FUNCTION) to display a message in the output window. When the Breakpoint is hit and the condition is met the message specified here will be written to the output window.

Figure 12 - Action on a condition

Since the "Continue Execution" box is checked the debugger will NOT stop but continue on. This provides for monitoring a Breakpoint and associated values without actually stopping the execution. Logically speaking this is form of output debugging as discussed earlier, but more control is given and the specifics of what to output are completely contained in the Breakpoint construct. Conversely if the checkbox is not set execution will stop like a normal breakpoint after performing the action.

This additional information on a breakpoint – the logging of a message when reached, is also sometimes referred to as a tracepoint. When right-clicking on a line of code there is an option for "Insert a Tracepoint"; this is essentially a shortcut for creating a breakpoint and then adding the additional logging information. Also, once the Action feature is used the icon will be a red diamond instead of a circle.

In Figure 9 there are two other useful options that do not fall into the control flow discussion but can be very useful when navigating large sections of code. These deal with locating where functions are called and are referenced. Both of these may help when inspecting call stacks during debugging or error analysis.

When clicking over a particular function, the View Call Hierarchy menu item will display the upward call paths to the function. This shows the possible ways that a method may be called. This is shown in Figure 13 for the simplified example project's `CalculateRandomDiscount()` function.

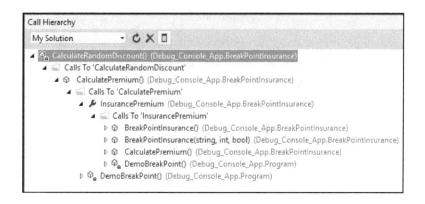

Figure 13 - Call Hierarchy Display

Find all References will present in list form all the places where the chosen function is called. Clicking each item in the list will go to that code location. This is a quick way to navigate and inspect the locations where a method is called and its surrounding statements.

Debugging Release Builds

The previous sections have discussed techniques for debugging code as it is being developed by the developer. This is a very important step and the enormous importance of it should not be overlooked. Numerous studies have found the earlier a defect is identified in the design/development/build/release/maintain application lifecycle the easier and cheaper it is to fix.

That being said, how is it that code that has been released to production can be investigated? In some organizations the end users may be available for a face-to-face meeting or a demonstration via a screen-sharing tool. But in many situations this is not the case. Software that is installed over the internet, shrink-wrapped games, or mobile applications are all examples of distribution methods where the developer will most likely not have the opportunity of direct feedback from the user. So when an error is reported or some problem identified how can the developer examine what the code actually did without debugging?

Logging is a common way to record actions in code to a persistent storage mechanism for possible inspection at a later time. Unlike the debugging output described earlier, these statements are meant to stay in release code and record statements to a dedicated resource. In some cases company policy or government regulation may require a log for security or audit purposes.

The storage mechanism can vary from a simple text file to a database table to a system event log such as the Windows Event Log. The format of the information can also vary widely. Access to the resource can vary as well depending on requirements and design.

Logging statements can be written in several ways. Simple output statements to a text would suffice, however the most common method is to use a logging framework. These too can be custom in-house, open source, or a third party component.

Additionally, the level of detail can vary widely. Simple code trace statements (i.e. "SomeFunction called") may be logged as well as detailed function/argument/condition statements. Some tools also have the ability to log different statements to different logs based on predetermined configuration. Some statements may go to a debug log, some to an information log, and some to an error log.

While there are several frameworks and packages available, the one that will be discussed and demonstrated here has been officially ported to many languages with many un-official ports as well. This demonstration is in no way meant to be an endorsement of this product over others available; rather it is an introduction to logging using a tool that should be easy to translate to other languages if needed.

Log4net is part of the Apache Logging Project (see bibliography). What was originally a logging framework for Java has been ported to .Net, C++, JavaScript, PHP, and many others. What is important here is that the terms/definitions, configuration, and output should be similar between them.

Installation in Visual Studio is done through the NuGet package manager. Simply choose to "Manage NuGet Packages" and search for Log4Net. Optionally the source and distribution can be downloaded from the Apache site and included as libraries but this is more difficult to maintain with updates.

Once the package has been added to a project, the first step is configuring the framework. In a Visual Studio project this is done in the .config file. Since log4net is not a built-in .net framework the first declaration is a reference to the library itself. Without going into a full explanation of the .net configuration syntax the XML in Listing 5 shows all that is needed. This does not define any debugging objects, it simply informs the .net framework that a custom configuration section will be defined later and it should be processed by the Log4Net configuration handler.

```
<configSections>
    <section name="log4net"
             type="log4net.Config.Log4NetConfigurationSectionHandler, log4net"
             requirePermission="false"/>
</configSections>
```

Listing 5

The actual debugging objects is what are described in the custom configuration section. As mentioned above there are many possibilities of where to log statements to – a database, a file, and system logs. A key term in the log4net world to represent this is the "Appender".

An "Appender" is where log messages are sent and appended to the end. There are several pre-defined by log4net, but the concept is interface-based and can be extended with custom user defined appenders if necessary. The full list, definitions, and available configurable properties are available on the logging.apache.org website; the following table describes some of the more commonly used appenders.

Appender Name	Description
AdoNetAppender	Sends entries to a database table. The Table must have a certain structure.
ConsoleAppender	Send entries to the output console.
EventLogAppender	Send entries to the Windows Event Log.
FileAppender	Send entries to a text file.
RollingFileAppender	Send entries to a text file that rolls based on size or date.
SmtpAppender	Send entries to an email recipient.

Table 1 – Sample Log Appenders

With each one of these Appenders there is a number of properties specific to that Appender. These can be configured as XML elements in each case; the handler will use the name of the element to set the name of the corresponding property.

Shown in Listing 6 is an example of the log4net section with one Appender defined. It is a RollingFileAppender with child elements used to configure the properties of the appender. The first six relate to the specifics of naming the file and how to roll it, in this case it will be rolled by date and since the datePattern ends in "HH" it will be rolled every hour. More specifics can be found in the RollingFileAppender documentation.

```
<log4net>
  <appender name="RollingAppender" type="log4net.Appender.RollingFileAppender">
    <file value="C:\projects\LOGS\DebugLogDemo.txt"/>
    <appendToFile value="true"/>
    <rollingStyle value="Date"/>
    <datePattern value="yyyyMMdd-HH" />
    <maxSizeRollBackups value="10"/>
    <staticLogFileName value="true"/>
    <layout type="log4net.Layout.PatternLayout">
      <header value="" />
      <footer value="" />
      <conversionPattern value="%d{MM-dd-yyyy::HH:mm:ss} | %-5p %c | %m %n" />
    </layout>
    <threshold value="Info" />
  </appender>
  <root>
    <appender-ref ref="RollingAppender" />
  </root>
</log4net>
```

Listing 6

A more complex element is the `layout` element. This element describes how the output will be written to the file. The `conversionPattern` element has a value that looks like an output statement. In fact it is; the statement will be transformed by the framework with populated values for output. Table 2 below summarizes the escape characters and their meaning.

Character	Transformation
%d	The date the log entry is written. Formatting for the date is specified within the {} brackets.
%p	The threshold value of the entry (detailed shortly).

%c	The class name of the logger; typically this is the class where the statement originated.
%m	The message specified by the logging statement.
%n	Newline constant

Table 2 – Conversion Pattern Specifiers

The last element under appender is `threshold`. This is a property common to all appenders and is how the framework determines which statements to log. It is often also referred to as the logging "level" as has several predefined values. In order from lowest to highest the values are All, Debug, Info, Warn, Error, Fatal, and Off.

These values are important for two reasons. One is that the methods of the log interface match the values by name. In short the `ILog.Debug()` method is used for debug messages, `ILog.Info()` is used for information messages, etc. This will be further demonstrated a little later when actual coding is shown.

The other reason is that the threshold value can be used for filtering and targeting multiple appenders. For simple filtering, whichever value the appender is set to, that value and all above will be included; all values below the specified value will not be processed. For further refinement a `<filter />` tag can be used which can be set to match only a single level. This allows for fine tuning and potentially a log scheme where an appender exists for each level.

Before demonstrating the advanced techniques of multiple appenders and filtering a simple code example of using the logger of Listing 6 and its output should be shown. While there are many different patterns of usage to logging a simple "log per class" will be demonstrated here. This involves having a static class variable that is instantiated with the value of the class where it is declared. For example in the top of the Program class would be the statement shown below:

```
static ILog _log = LogManager.GetLogger(
                         typeof(Program));
```

Listing 7 - Declaring a Logger

Each class where logging is desired would have a declaration like this, each with its own typeof(className) value. Then throughout the class the _log variable could be used for sending messages to the log. This is shown in Listing 8.

The output is shown below in Figure 14. Notice that the output follows the format described previously. Also note that the Debug statement does not show up as the threshold of the appender is above the Debug level.

Finally, Figure 15 shows the contents in the Logs folder. Notice how the files are very small but have been "rolled" according to date/time. The previous files have been renamed to have their respective date/time appended to the filename. Comparing the filenames with the code in Listing 6 will show how the name is derived.

```
1   01-02-2018::20:30:23  |  INFO   Debug_Console_App.Program  |  Calculating Insuance Premium
2   01-02-2018::20:30:24  |  INFO   Debug_Console_App.Program  |  Premium calculated for Tommy Trouble as 992
3
```

Figure 14 - Output File Content

```
static void DemoBreakPoint()
{
  Console.WriteLine("Calculating insurance premium");
  _log.Info("Calculating Insuance Premium");
  _log.Debug("This should not show up in file
              due to filter");

  BreakPointInsurance bpi = new BreakPointInsurance(
                                "Tommy Trouble",
                                20, true);
  bpi.CalculatePremium();

  Console.WriteLine("Driver " + bpi.Name + ", age " +
                bpi.Age + ", pays a premium of " +
                bpi.InsurancePremium);
  _log.Info("Premium calculated for " + bpi.Name +
            " as " + bpi.InsurancePremium);
}
```

Listing 8 - Using the _log Variable

DebugLogDemo.txt	1 KB	1/2/2018 8:30 PM	Text Document
DebugLogDemo.txt20180101-18	1 KB	1/1/2018 6:34 PM	TXT20180101-18 File
DebugLogDemo.txt20180101-17	1 KB	1/1/2018 5:06 PM	TXT20180101-17 File

Figure 15 - Example of rolled files.

With the simple debug statements and configuration shown previously, now is the time to discuss multiple loggers and using filters and the threshold property. As mentioned earlier, the threshold element specifies the level at which an appender receives and processes log statements.

Another appender could be created and added to the file in Listing 6. If it was exactly the same as the appender already there (with only a different filename) and a Threshold value of "Debug" then the debug statements would be sent to that log also.

```xml
<!-- previous appender definition -->
</appender>
<appender name="RollingDebugAppender"
      type="log4net.Appender.RollingFileAppender">
  <file value="C:\projects\LOGS\DebugLevelLog.txt"/>
  <!-- values removed for brevity -->
  <threshold value="Debug" />
</appender>
<root>
  <appender-ref ref="RollingAppender" />
  <appender-ref ref="RollingDebugAppender" />
</root>
```

Listing 9 - Additional Appender Definition

This can be done for each and every logging level to have an appender for each level. But there is a little bit of a problem with that approach. Because each threshold includes itself and all levels above, the Debug log will contain (in this example) both Debug and Info statements, while the original appender only contains Info-level statements.

This isn't truly a "log per level." Rather it is a logging system that becomes narrower with each log. While this may be OK in some cases it can also be repetitive and use a lot of unnecessary space. Through the use of filtering a more specific logging can be implemented.

There are several filters in the log4net framework. The only one demonstrated here will be the `LevelMatchFilter`; the reader is encouraged to look at the other filters. This filter will match to an individual level and when combined with the `DenyAll` filter will only log the matched level events. Listing 10 shows a snippet of a definition for an appender that only accepts Warn log events. These would be sent with the `ILog.Warn()` method.

```
<!-- previous appender definitions -->
</appender>
<appender name="WarnOnlyAppender"
    type="log4net.Appender.RollingFileAppender">
  <file value="C:\projects\LOGS\WarningOnly.txt"/>
  <!-- values removed for brevity -->
  <filter type="log4net.Filter.LevelMatchFilter">
      <levelToMatch value="Warn" />
  </filter>
  <filter type="log4net.Filter.DenyAllFilter" />
</appender>
<root>
  <appender-ref ref="RollingAppender" />
  <appender-ref ref="RollingDebugAppender" />
  <appender-ref ref="WarnOnlyAppender" />
</root>
```

Listing 10 - Filter for Matching Specific Level

Using multiple log files can be most beneficial when isolating different types of logging statements is desired. Different file names be used as in Listings 9 and 10 and this can easily segregate errors by level. Information, Debug, Warning, and Errors can all be in different files so that inspecting each is easier.

Even different methods could be employed. This is ideal when immediate notification is desired, such as an email alert on an error that is determined to be extremely critical. Logging can be used in conjunction with standard exception handling to present the developer with detailed information around an issue.

Exceptions, the exception framework, and the discussions around their proper usage are outside the scope of this book. For purposes here it is enough to say that Exceptions are "thrown" by .Net in situations where the Framework itself encounters errors. The discussion that follows is for demonstrating how they can be used in logging. As with all the examples the logic and output is both a bit contrived and over simplified, but the principles can be easily scaled and applied to real applications.

The code in Listing 11 is a method added to the `BreakPointInsurance` class to save a premium statement to a file. It shows the usage of multiple levels of logging as previously discussed. New is the use of exception properties for detailed error statements. The `Message` and `StackTrace` properties of the `Exception` class contain information that the developer can use to help trace problem.

```
public void SaveQuoteToFile(String path,
                            String fileName )
{
  if (String.IsNullOrEmpty(fileName))
  {
    _log.Warn("No file name provided - cannot save");
    return;
  }

  _log.Info("Saving quote to " + path + fileName);

  try
  {
    TextWriter tw = File.CreateText(path + fileName);
    tw.WriteLine("Driver: " + this.Name);
    tw.WriteLine("Years Experience: " +
                 this.YearsDriving);
    tw.WriteLine("Number of tickets: " +
                 this.SpeedingTickts);
    tw.WriteLine("Premium: $" +
                 this.InsurancePremium);

    tw.Close();
  }
  catch(Exception e)
  {
    _log.Error("Exception writing to file: " +
               e.Message);
    _log.Error("Stack Trace: " + e.StackTrace);

  }
}
```

Listing 11 - Logging and Exceptions

Quickly looking at the code it can be seen that there are three paths through the code. In the first path a file name is not provided and the function writes a warning message and immediately exits. In the second the file is successfully opened, written to, closed, and the function exits. This is sometimes referred to as the "happy path" for obvious reasons. The third path is if the output file cannot be opened, an exception is thrown, the details logged, and the function exits. Since this is a void function and returns no value, the calling code has no way to know what made the function return. If the developer has to investigate why an output file is not being created the log statements can help determine which code path is being followed.

The code shown in Listing 12 is used to call the `SaveQuoteToFile` method and demonstrates each of these code paths. Output from the two non-exception paths would appear as before in the appropriate files. Recall there was a Debug level file and a Warning-specific file. In the current configuration (Listing 10) there isn't an Error-specific file, so the error statements would appear in the Debug log file with a level of Error.

The output statements are shown in Figure 16 (wrapped so it fits on the screen – not pretty but readable). The `Message` is a short user-friendly summary of the problem; is this case the specified path cannot be found. This gives the developer an idea of the problem. Combined with other statements and normal debugging procedures this may often be sufficient to locate the problem. There can also be conventions employed such as including the name of the method or some other identifying information in the output. Or including additional properties of the `Exception` class that are not discussed here.

```
// Good call:
String fileName = bpi.Name + "_quote.txt";
String filePath = @"C:\projects\LOGS\";
bpi.SaveQuoteToFile(filePath, fileName);

// Empty call
bpi.SaveQuoteToFile("", "");

// Exception Call
bpi.SaveQuoteToFile(@"c:\projects\LOGSSS\",
                    "path-non-exist.txt");
```

Listing 12 - Code to Demonstrate Exception Logging

The second ERROR statement is the log output in Figure 16 is the output of the `StackTrace` parameter. This is much more detailed and describes exactly where the error occurred, from the system-level code on line 9 (`System.IO.__Error`) all the way up to the user code at line 16 (`BreakPointExample.cs:line 136`). In this simple example there is only one level of user code but in a real-world example there may be several. This detailed information can be of great use to the developer in researching error conditions reported by users.

```
7   01-07-2018::10:20:44 | INFO  Debug_Console_App.BreakPointInsurance |
    Saving quote to c:\projects\LOGSSS\path-non-exist.txt
8   01-07-2018::10:20:57 | ERROR Debug_Console_App.BreakPointInsurance |
    Exception writing to file: Could not find a part of the path
    'c:\projects\LOGSSS\path-non-exist.txt'.
9   01-07-2018::10:20:59 | ERROR Debug_Console_App.BreakPointInsurance |
    Stack Trace:    at System.IO._Error.WinIOError(Int32 errorCode,
    String maybeFullPath)
10     at System.IO.FileStream.Init(String path, FileMode mode, FileAccess
       access, Int32 rights, Boolean useRights, FileShare share, Int32
       bufferSize, FileOptions options, SECURITY_ATTRIBUTES secAttrs,
       String msgPath, Boolean bFromProxy, Boolean useLongPath, Boolean
       checkHost)
11     at System.IO.FileStream..ctor(String path, FileMode mode,
       FileAccess access, FileShare share, Int32 bufferSize, FileOptions
       options, String msgPath, Boolean bFromProxy, Boolean useLongPath,
       Boolean checkHost)
12     at System.IO.StreamWriter.CreateFile(String path, Boolean append,
       Boolean checkHost)
13     at System.IO.StreamWriter..ctor(String path, Boolean append,
       Encoding encoding, Int32 bufferSize, Boolean checkHost)
14     at System.IO.StreamWriter..ctor(String path, Boolean append)
15     at System.IO.File.CreateText(String path)
16     at Debug_Console_App.BreakPointInsurance.SaveQuoteToFile(String
       path, String fileName) in C:\Users\ecrookshanks\Documents\PSDT
       book\Just Enough Series\Source
       Code\Debug_Console_App\Debug_Console_App\BreakPointExample.cs:line
       136
17
```

Figure 16- Exception Logging Output

Summary

Debugging is an integral part of software development.
Modern IDEs such as Visual Studio have an array of options
available that go far beyond the original methods of simple
output. While that is still possible in small applications or in
certain application circumstances the use of breakpoints,
stepping, the immediate window, and flow control
statements gives the developer much more control and
much less invasive ways to debug code.

The previous section demonstrated many tools and techniques that are commonly used in the author's experience. But there may be many other approaches for debugging including different standards or conventions or even organizational restrictions. Although popular, the log4net framework is an open source non-standard framework. Microsoft has a similar proprietary framework that might be dictated to be used; it may also be required to use a custom in-house developed logging mechanism. Policy, product, and platform may also dictate where logging occurs. Local file, database, email, and system log may be off limits or impractical in some applications.

Whatever the limitations or frameworks involved the previous discussion and demonstrations should be applicable in some form or fashion. Understanding the capabilities and methods should also improve the code quality even if certain tools are unavailable.

Unit Testing

Unit testing is code testing that is done by the developer. In conjunction with debugging this is the primary way a developer ensures that the code is functioning properly. And also similar to debugging, techniques and tools have also evolved.

Initially unit testing was primarily done manually; normally with a set of functions that exercised a section of code and produced results that would be compared with a set of known expected results. The code was either in a separate project or conditionally compiled with the main source. As with debug statements these would have been in place for debug code and removed for production releases. What is tested could be as small as a single function, a class interface, or even an entire module or program.

Automated testing is very common now, for two reasons. One is that, just like logging, there are several frameworks and tools that exist for testing. Similar to log4net there is a suite of related tools known collectively as "xUnit". nUnit for .NET, jUnit for Java, jsUnit for JavaScript, etc. Vendors such as Microsoft also have integrated testing frameworks. Most of these have a common or very similar terminology and tools that integrate into development environments. There are also stand-alone tools and tools that integrate into build environments. The latter allows automated testing to be part of the continuous integration process. A testing framework will be discussed and demonstrated later in this section.

The second reason is the emergence of a development methodology known as Test Driven Development, or TDD. A complete discussion of this methodology is beyond the scope of this book. However a summary is important both for this section and the Refactoring section that is next.

For any new feature developed in TDD a test is written first. For example if we have a requirement to write a function that takes three numeric inputs and returns the product of the first two raised to the power of the third. What follows is the process for each step.

Task	Logical Result
Write a test for the `ProductPower()` function.	`ProductPower(2,2,2) == 16?`
Run the test(s)	Code will not compile because `ProductPower()` function does not exist.

Write stub for ProductPower()	`int ProductPower(`
	`int x, int y, int z)`
	`{`
	`    return 0;`
	`}`

Run the test(s)	Test fails because 0 not equal to 16.

Implement the function just enough to make it pass the test.	`int ProductPower(`
	`int x, int y, int z)`
	`{`
	`    return (x*y)^z;`
	`}`

Run the test(s)	Test(s) succeed.

Developing a new piece of software using this method might seem a little strange. Why write a test that will not compile? Why only code enough to make it compile and fail, and then only enough to make it pass?

Again, there are many more in-depth resources that discuss TDD so all the reasons and rationale will not be outlined here. The main reason highlighted here will be that TDD allows the developer to be confident that once a test is successful any further modifications or changes to the code can be instantly checked to make sure that nothing breaks. This is especially useful in complex methods that rely on other functions or libraries for part of their processing.

Another supplemental reason is how TDD ties into the topic of refactoring. As elaborated on in the next section, refactoring is the process of changing code to be more readable, more efficient, better organized, etc. When using TDD to develop functionality a principal that is often applied is "do the simplest thing that will work." The logical example expressed this as coding "just enough to make the test pass."

However it is phrased the "simple first" design of TDD practically ensures that the code will change as the design evolves. For example, if a collection of variables is needed the simplest construct to use is an array. So complete the code with an array. As the design evolves this could change to be a built-in collection (such as List or Queue) or could be a brand new class. Either way once a test is in place it would ensure that any changes to the collection mechanism would not change the outward results of the test.

Finally, before an example of a testing framework with actual code is shown the question of "What to test?" should be answered. Surprisingly this is sometimes a contentious question as some believe that everything should be tested while some believe in omitting certain areas for various reasons. The areas of contention will be discussed and highlighted below. The goal here is not to take a side on these discussions but to present the arguments that might be heard.

Property testing is one of these areas. These are also known as "getters and setters" because they are usually simple `"return val"` or `"property = val"` single line statements. In .NET these are also sometimes coded in a class as simple `Property {get; set;}` statements and the backing implementation is inserted by the compiler. Writing tests for these properties are often left out due to their simplicity and the fact that the testing code would be larger than the code being tested.

On the other hand, sometimes properties are not simple and may include verification checks such as a null or valid-value tests. In this case writing tests for only these non-simple properties may be in order. It could then be argued that this approach could be a maintenance hassle as some properties are tested while others are not. It could also be argued that these validity checks should not be in simple properties. So there are many arguments here and the answer could vary between organizations.

Another area of discussion is User Interface testing, whether for web-based or desktop applications. One reason this is questioned is because there can be many answers to the question of "What is to be tested in the GUI?" As will be seen later in code most unit test frameworks use Boolean assertions to compare expected and actual values. Adapting those to a User Interface object is not always easy or even apparent how to test.

In some cases Unit Tests are written for UIs to ensure they are properly initiated through various properties or values. These could be whether or not a control's `Visible` or `Enabled` property is properly set. In a web-based application a page might be tested to see if the session is initiated correctly, or if the page posts to appropriate URL when submitted. In a logical sense this is testing a GUI as a plain object rather than testing the true appearance or layout.

There are UI testing frameworks available but those will not be discussed here. These exist for Windows, web-based, and mobile applications and can be quite extensive. Some will test state as discussed above and some also will verify screen content and layout/arrangement. The decision on whether or not to use these would largely be product and organization specific.

Testing Framework

As noted previously there are several testing frameworks. Because it is built in to Visual Studio, the following demonstration will use the Microsoft Testing Framework, sometimes referred to as MSTest. There will also be a brief discussion at the end comparing the terminology and usage with the nUnit tool. All of the concepts are very similar but there are minor terminology differences between the frameworks as well as differences in displaying results.

The most common and preferred way to test code with Visual Studio is through the use of a test project. This project can then reference other projects in the solution and can be given access to use other classes and entities. This cleanly separates "core" code such as data access, business logic, and GUI projects from the testing project. The following demonstration will add a test project and several unit tests to the project used in the debugging section.

To add a test project to the solution, ensure the solution is selected and right-click on it. From the context menu choose "Add ->New Project", find the "Test" project category and choose "Unit Test Project" shown below in Figure 17.

Figure 17 - Unit Test Project Type

Once the project is added there will now be two (or more) projects in the solution as shown in Figure 18. It is important to note that this will not affect any of the debugging statements made so far. When running the application the main project is still the "startup" project and is shown in bold. Pressing F5 or clicking the "run" button will continue to function as before; testing is done through another menu altogether.

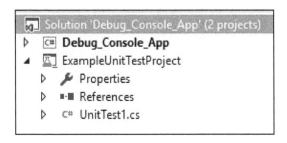

Figure 18 - Main and Testing Projects

When created the project will create one test class as shown above. By default this is "UnitTest1" and contains starter code. Before using and modifying the starter code it is a necessary to add the reference to the code being tested. In the case of Figure 18 this is obvious as there is only one other project in the solution. However as mentioned previously there could be several other projects such as data access library projects, business logic projects, GUI projects, etc. This is done by right-clicking on "References" and following the standard method to add a reference to an entire project or a particular class to be tested.

The template code created by adding the project is shown in Listing 13. Each aspect of the template will be explained before adding actual test code.

```
namespace ExampleUnitTestProject
{
    [TestClass]
    public class UnitTest1
    {
        [TestMethod]
        public void TestMethod1()
        {
        }
    }
}
```

Listing 13 - Template Test Code

The first two items to discuss are the attributes on the class and the method. The `TestClass` attribute identifies the class as one that contains tests. The `TestMethod` attribute identifies a method that is to serve as a test. These attributes inform the test framework of which items will be part of the test. Note something important: there is no `main` method or any other obvious entry point for this project. In fact the framework will treats this as a library class; the attributes are the only way of informing the framework which methods are test methods. Other important attributes will be discussed later when more code is written.

Both the class name and test method name are important. When the tests are run they will be shown in the results pane by name. Changing `UnitTest1` and `TestMethod1` to more meaningful names is a best practice. After renaming the class and test name and writing an actual test, the code is shown in Listing 14.

```
[TestClass]
public class BreakPointInsuranceTests
{
    [TestMethod]
    public void TestNonZeroPremium()
    {
        // No arg constructor sets premium to 0
        BreakPointInsurance bpi = new
                        BreakPointInsurance();
        // should calculate premium
        int prem = bpi.InsurancePremium;

        Assert.AreNotEqual(0, prem);

    }
}
```

Listing 14 - Updated Test Class and Method

For this simple test an instance of the class under test is created and a property value is accessed. The comments are there to explain the logic – accessing the property should result in the insurance premium being calculated. This is checked by use of the testing framework's `Assert` class and `AreNotEqual` method. These will be discussed in more detail shortly.

There are several ways to run unit tests. Using the Test menu is a very common way; this involves selecting Test->Run->All Tests. Another way is to open the Test Explorer window from the Test->Windows->Test Explorer. When running and re-running tests a common way is to open the Test Explorer and leave it open as a tabbed window. This is shown below in Figure 19.

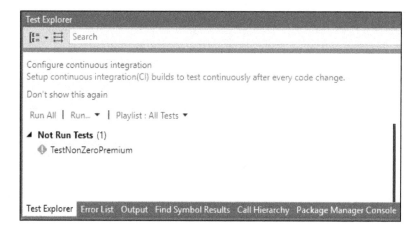

Figure 19 - Test Explorer Window

This window is very informative and useful. Based on the attributes in the code it knows about the tests that are present in the testing project. It also shows that they have not been run yet. The display allows for grouping and sorting tests by different selections; clicking on the grouping button at the top left allows for grouping tests by class, duration, outcome, trait (such as category) or test project. The tests can all be run at once (Run All) or using the dropdown to choose to run Failed, Not Run, or Passed tests, or to repeat the last run.

With a single test, running the test will change the display to that shown in Figure 20.

Figure 20 - Passed Test and Summary

Before writing more tests the `Assert` class and its testing methods should be explained. `Assert` is a static class with all static methods. The `AreNotEqual` method was shown in Listing 14, but this is just one of several overridden methods used in unit testing. The following table summarizes the methods. In general each method may have several overrides for different sets of inputs. Details of all the possible overrides are documented more thoroughly on MSDN.

Assertion Method	Notes
AreEqual	Check if the inputs are equal, either by value or by reference.
AreNotEqual	Check if the inputs are not equal, either by value or by reference.
AreNotSame	Check to see if the object inputs do not reference the same object.

AreSame	Check to see if the object inputs do reference the same object.
Equals	Checks if the two object inputs are equal.
IsFalse	Checks if an input Boolean value/expression is false.
IsInstanceOfType	Checks if the input object matches a specified input type.
IsNotInstanceOfType	Checks if the input object does not match a specified input type.
IsNotNull	Checks if the input object is non null.
IsNull	Checks if the input object is null.
IsTrue	Checks if an input Boolean value/expression is true.

All of these methods are declared as `void` and return no value. When the check "fails" an exception is thrown; the exception is caught by the framework on a per-method basis and this is how the framework reports a failed test.

There is no limit to the number of test methods a particular test class can have. There are different rules of thumb for how test classes and actual classes match up. These may vary from enterprise to enterprise or even project to project. The discussion here is not enter into that argument, only to demonstrate the syntax, tools, methods, and useability.

To show how a failed test looks a simple test was written with a single failing statement. The statement is shown below in Listing 15 with the Test Explorer output shown in Figure 21. Note that the IsTrue override being used includes both a Boolean expression and a string message to be displayed on failure. This is a common override for many of the assertion methods shown previously; an addition string parameter to be displayed when the test fails.

```
[TestMethod]
public void AnExampleFailTest()
{
    Assert.IsTrue(1==0, "This is a fail message");
}
```

Listing 15 - Failing method with Fail Message

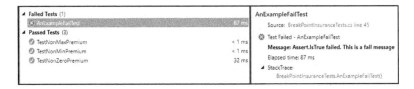

Figure 21 - Failing test with a Message

Looking at the test code in Listing 14 it can be seen that an instance of the class under test, BreakPointInsurance, is instantiated in the test method. While this is fine for the simple coding test here, there are other ways to instantiate objects that are cleaner and more extensible.

The easiest way to reliably initialize variables is to use class variables and create a method to instantiate and configure those variables. That method can then be marked with the [TestInitialize] attribute. This method will then be called before every test method executes.

```
BreakPointInsurance testBPI;

[TestInitialize]
public void InitTest()
{
    // No arg constructor sets premium to 0
    testBPI = new BreakPointInsurance();
}

[TestMethod]
public void TestNonZeroPremium()
{
    // access property should calculate premium
    int prem = testBPI.InsurancePremium;

    Assert.AreNotEqual(0, prem);
}
```

Listing 16 - TestInitialize and Class Variables

In Listing 16 the `InitTest` method will be called before each test method is executed. Therefore each test shown in Figure 21 will not need to create its own instance of `BreakPointInsurance` unless it specifically needs to. Rather it can use the class instance to exercise methods and access properties as the `TestNonZeroPremium` test does. This also has the added benefit that each test starts with an instance in the same state.

There is also a `TestCleanup` attribute that can be applied to a method that will run after every test. This method can be used to perform clean-up steps after each run. There is no need for this for the tests in the previous code. However if the initialization method had allocated resources that are not automatically reclaimed, such as database connections, file handles, or other system resources, the clean-up method would need to dispose of those.

At a higher level there are also `ClassInitialize/ClassCleanup` attributes and `AssemblyInitialize/AssemblyCleanup` attributes that apply to the class and assembly levels respectively. These identify methods that would be executed only once at their respective levels. The limiting factor is that the methods with these attributes are required to be declared `static` so there is no access to the non-static class variables. However if a class made use of static variables or other constructs they could easily be initialized and disposed of through these functions.

One other attribute commonly used is `TestCategory`. This is purely to give a test a category name. Then tests can be grouped together in the Test Explorer window. Listing 17 shows this attribute usage with Figure 22 showing the resultant Test Explorer window after grouping by trait.

```
[TestMethod]
[TestCategory("Premium")]
public void TestNonZeroPremium()
{}

[TestMethod]
[TestCategory("Premium_Max")]
public void TestNonMaxPremium()
{}

[TestMethod]
[TestCategory("Premium")]
public void TestNonMinPremium()
{}
```

Listing 17- TestCategory Attribute

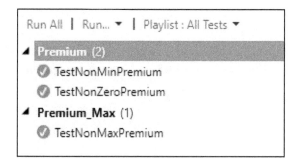

Figure 22 - Grouping by Category Name

NUnit

The previous section demonstrated the use of the Microsoft Testing Framework integrated into Visual Studio. As the "?Unit" family of testing frameworks is also popular this section will briefly discuss both how they are similar and how they differ from the Microsoft framework. Note that the discussion here will be limited to NUnit as a direct comparison to MSTest. JUnit, CPPUnit, etc. will be similar but will not be shown here.

As with MSTest, an NUnit testing project is a separate library project within a solution. However rather than adding a "Unit Test Project" as before, a simple "Class Library" project is added. This is the first hint that NUnit is not tightly integrated with Visual Studio by default.

Once the project is added, the easiest way to include the testing framework is to use the Nuget Package Manager. Adding the NUnit package to the project will include the correct references. Once the NUnit namespace is included in the class the same tests as before coded for NUnit are shown in Listing 18.

Notice that other than slight differences in the attribute names the code is essentially the same as MSTest. Use of Intellisense and checking the documentation will reveal that there are not as many overloads in the NUNit `Assert` class as in the corresponding MSTest `Assert`. However the results are the same.

```
[TestFixture]
public class NUnitTests
{
    private BreakPointInsurance testBPI;

    [SetUp]
    public void SetUpObjects()
    {
        testBPI = new BreakPointInsurance();
    }

    [TestCase]
    [Category("NUnit Legacy Syntax")]
    public void TestAutoCalculatePremium()
    {
        int prem = testBPI.InsurancePremium;

        Assert.AreNotEqual(0, prem);
    }
}
```

Listing 18 - Tests in the NUnit Framework (Legacy)

Newer versions of NUnit also have an additional way of
using assertions. A that() method with various constraint
objects and multiple overloads. This is shown in Listing 19
but due to its quite obvious syntax difference will not be
explored any further here. It should however be noted that
instead of multiple Equal/NotEqual/Null, etc methods for
checking values, the complexity now moves to the
constraint expression. This is also extensible in that custom
expressions may be developed and used. More information
is available on the NUnit Github site (see bibliography).

```
Assert.That(prem, Is.Not.EqualTo(0));
```

Listing 19 - Newer NUnit Assertion

To run and view the results of the NUnit tests there are a couple of options. One is to use a test runner tool that is separate from Visual Studio. There a several forms of this tool including a command-line runner and a Windows GUI executable. In both of these the individual project that is the NUnit test project must be loaded and referenced.

At the time of this writing the GUI test tool is being rewritten and is still in Beta. It can be downloaded from GitHub. The command line tool will execute all tests in the project, display the results of individual tests, and print a summary. The output is color-coded for easy reference. Additionally an XML file is output so that if needed it could be read and processed as a report using XSLT or other tools.

There is also an NUnit adapter/extension for Visual Studio. This allows NUnit tests to be run in the built-in Test Explorer. The extension is installed via the normal Visual Studio extension tools menu. Once installed the NUnit tests appear as normal tests in the Test Explorer and the same groupings and functions apply. Once these tools are in place writing and maintaining an NUnit test project is no different than using the built-in framework. Organizations may favor one or the other based on performance or interoperability with other languages but other than setup steps the usage is practically identical.

Mocks

One final discussion on testing concerns the use of mock objects. This is high level overview discussion here because the use of mock objects is often combined with a specific design pattern and design patterns are out of scope for this book. Design Patterns are discussed in another "Just Enough" series book.

In a normal multi-tiered application there are boundaries between layers and components. There may be a data-access layer that directly queries the database, a business layer that implements business rules, and a GUI layer that consists of the web pages and/or desktop application. Even within these layers there may be distinct components written in an effort to reduce change impact. In an enterprise application there can also be communication with other systems that may take place through remote procedure calls, web services, or message queueing.

Using the actual external systems or dependant components is often not desirable or even possible during unit testing. External systems may not be available at the time of development or may be inaccessible due to security. An application's database is usually available, however tests that modify or alter data are usually not optimal. Those modifications may have to be cleaned up so the test would start in a known state each time and not affect other areas of the application's testing.

Coding a system capable of using mock objects generally involves design patterns known as Dependency Injection (DI), Factory Methods, or Service Repository combined with the practice of coding to interfaces. Again, a thorough discussion of this is beyond the scope of this book, but a very brief introduction is given next for demonstrating mock testing.

In Listing 16 the test function creates a new instance of the `BreakPointInsurance` class for testing by allocating it with `new`. In a large enterprise system this most likely would not be the case. One way would be for the client tier to work with a service layer that would retrieve a `BreakPointInsurance` object from a repository. The service layer would be for implementing business logic operations while the repository layer handles data access. Changes to each layer would be isolated from the other layers. It also allows for the code to be easily tested using mock objects.

The following code snippets will show a very simple service class and repository interface. The service class will contain one method which will be tested. The mock objects created during the unit test will also be shown and described; a "real" implementation of the repository is not shown here.

The `IRepository` interface represents the storage mechanism for the system. In a real system this would contain methods for accessing all the different objects in the system. The simple system here only has a single type of object (`BreakPointInsurnace`) and for simplicity there are only two methods defined; a full implementation could have similar methods for each type of object in the system. This is shown in Listing 20.

```
public interface IRepository
{
    BreakPointInsurance GetPolicyById(int PolicyID);

    void UpdatePolicy(BreakPointInsurance Policy);

}
```

Listing 20 - Simple Repository Interface

The IRepository interface is used by the service class, InsuranceService, shown in Listing 21. It keeps a reference to an instance of the interface which is set in the constructor of the class. Thus when an instance of the InsuranceService class is created, the code creating the service passes in a reference to class that implements IRepository. InsuranceService does not know or care about the actual class serving as the repository as long as it implements the interface.

As noted before, in a large multi-tier application it would the client tier such as a web interface or a mobile application that would use the service class. The client tier could decide what type of repository to use and then pass that to the service. In the case of Unit Testing, the test itself is a "client" of the service layer and can decide to use a mock repository.

```
public class InsuranceService
{
    IRepository m_InsRepository = null;

    public InsuranceService(IRepository repo)
    {
        m_InsRepository = repo;
    }

    public BreakPointInsurance GetInsurancePolicy(
                                int PolicyID)
    {
        BreakPointInsurance bpi =
            m_InsRepository.GetPolicyById(PolicyID);

        return bpi;

    }

    public void DiscountPremium(
                    BreakPointInsurance Policy,
                    int Percent)
    {
        int currentPrem = Policy.InsurancePremium;
        double dblPerent = 1 -(Percent / 100.0);

        int newPrem = (int)(dblPerent*currentPrem);

        Policy.InsurancePremium = newPrem;

        m_InsRepository.UpdatePolicy(Policy);

    }
}
```

Listing 21 - Service Class

In Listing 21 the implementation of DiscountPremium takes an existing premium object and discounts its existing premium, saving the updated policy. Notice how it uses the class IRepository instance to accomplish these tasks. With an actual repository instance it would be updated in the database or whatever backing store is used. For repetitive tests this could be a problem.

Instead the Unit Test project uses a repository class that it is free to define. This class can make use of non-persistent storage and use set values to create repeatable tests. This is shown in List 22. For this simple test the TestingRepository class serves as a full implementation of the IRepository interface. For storage it uses a simple class-level variable and sets it to have known values in the constructor. Since there is only one the incoming ID value can be safely ignored. Updating the value through the repository is simply setting the class-level variable to the new instance.

The complete unit test using NUnit and the mock repository is shown in Listing 23. Notice the IRepository variable is set to an instance of TestingRepository, and that variable is used in the constructor of the InsuranceService variable.

```
public class TestingRepository : IRepository
{
    BreakPointInsurance m_policy = null;

    public TestingRepository()
    {
        m_policy = new BreakPointInsurance();
        m_policy.InsurancePremium = 800;
    }

    public BreakPointInsurance GetPolicyById(
                            int PolicyID)
    {
        return m_policy;
    }

    public void UpdatePolicy(
                BreakPointInsurance Policy)
    {
        m_policy = Policy;
    }
}
```

Listing 22 - Test IRepository Implementation

```
[TestClass]
public class TestWithMock
{
    IRepository ir = new TestingRepository();
    InsuranceService svc = null;

    [TestInitialize]
    public void InitTest()
    {
        svc = new InsuranceService(ir);
    }

    [TestMethod]
    public void TestDiscountPremium()
    {
        BreakPointInsurance bpi =
                        svc.GetInsurancePolicy(1);
        int before = bpi.InsurancePremium;
        Assert.AreEqual(800, before,
                    "Unexpected Starting Value");

        svc.DiscountPremium(bpi, 10);
        bpi = svc.GetInsurancePolicy(1);
        int after = bpi.InsurancePremium;

        Assert.AreEqual(720, after);

    }
}
```

Listing 23 - Unit Test using Mock Objects

Unit Testing Summary

The discussion of Unit Testing is meant to be a brief and mainly syntax-driven overview of what might be seen in an environment where testing is formalized. Test Driven Development was briefly discussed and this obviously results in Unit Tests. However many non-TDD environments use Unit Testing as well. This can for brand new code, enhancement of existing code, or in bug fixing.

Two examples of testing frameworks were shown, The Microsoft Testing Framework and NUnit. The attribute syntax and usage was similar between the two but the degree and ease of integration was different. These examples would be very similar to other frameworks. And although not discussed here, many of these integrate with continuous build frameworks that enable testing to be run as part of the formal build/release process.

Using mock objects for testing was shown along with a very brief introduction to the design patterns and enterprise coding architecture that allows them to be used. Not shown was an example of any mock testing framework. These exist and have different ways of integrating into the Unit Tests. The manual example shown with the simple test implementation of an interface is ample enough to demonstrate the concept. Since the frameworks may have many different ways of operating they were not shown.

Please refer to the bibliography for additional reading on Unit Testing, both for TDD and non-TDD environments.

Refactoring

In simplest terms, "Refactoring" is a fancy term for cleaning up code. But it is also more than that, especially in the realm of Test Driven Development and other Agile Methodologies. In these frameworks frequent code and extensibility are part of a rapid and continuous design environment. While the "cleaning up" aspect of refactoring certainly applies at times there is also the aspect of an evolving design.

The following discussion highlights both of these aspects with examples using Visual Studio and C#. Many development IDEs have similar capabilities in terms of automated support, but design evolution sometimes stretches the capability of automated tools. Code examples will be shown as well.

It should be noted that both debugging and unit testing are important when refactoring, hence why these three topics are grouped together in a single book. Debugging is important when trying to track down a change that caused code to break; unit testing is important for catching code early as soon as it breaks.

Many of the concepts discussed in this section (and many others) are explained in greater detail in what is often referred to as the single most important book on refactoring: *Refactoring: Improving the Design of Existing Code* by Martin Fowler, et al. (1999). Many have expanded on the topic since then but this was one of the first and the most often referenced works.

Refactoring to "clean up" code is important for several reasons as well as a little bit of a misnomer. The code does appear to be cleaner but this is really as a result of the refactoring not its main purpose. The main purpose of refactoring code is to change the inner workings of the code to make it easier to maintain, understand, extend in the future, and reduce duplication and clutter. All this without changing the outward functionality to the calling code, hence the frequent combination of unit tests.

The reader may reference a list of refactorings in [Fowler], as well as the expanded list found on refactoring.com website [Refactoring]. These are listed as named methods and a few will be demonstrated in the following demonstration. Note that the while the methods are generally named they may be carried out either manually (typing or cut-and-paste) or by use of a command within the IDE; the command may or may not match up with the official refactoring name.

Also note that the demonstration will be quite code and snapshot heavy. So while the discussion may appear to be long and in-depth the reality is that only a few refactoring techniques and commands are being shown. They will be the most common and their benefits will be immediately obvious but this is far from a complete discussion of all the tools and techniques of refactoring.

The code in List 24 is a method that is designed to return a complete insurance premium statement. The insurance class referenced is an expanded version of the `BreakPointInsurance` class used in several examples earlier. In the updated class a `Policy` has a policy number, an effective date, an expiration date, can have multiple members, and have multiple vehicles of different types.

```
public String PrintStatement()
{
    String statement = "";

    double total1;
    double total2;
    double total3;
    double total4;

    int cars;
    int motorcycles;
    int rvs;

    total1 = 0.0;
    foreach(Insurable ins in policy.Autos)
    {
        total1 += ins.VehicleValue *
                Insurable.AUTO_RATE;
    }

    total2 = 0.0;
    foreach (Insurable ins in
                policy.Motorcycles)
    {
        total2 += ins.VehicleValue *
                Insurable.MOTOR_RATE;
    }
```

```
total3 = 0.0;
foreach (Insurable ins in policy.RVs)
{
    total3 += ins.VehicleValue +
             Insurable.RV_RATE;
}

total4 = 0.0;
foreach (Person p in policy.People)
{
    total4 += p.BasePremium;
}

// Find policy total
Double totalAmount = total1 + total2 +
                    total3 + total4;
Double tax = totalAmount * 0.05;

Double grossTotal = totalAmount + tax;

// Find the number of high risk Drivers
int risky = 0;
foreach (Person p in policy.People)
{
    if ( p.Age < 25)
    {
        riskyTmp += 1;
    }
}

// Get Policy details - name, ID
String PolicyID = policy.PolicyNumber;
String PolicyHolder = "None Specified";
foreach (Person p in policy.People)
{
    if (p.IsPolicyHolder)
    {
        PolicyHolder = p.FullName;
        break;
    }
}
```

```
statement = "Insurance Policy: " + PolicyID +
            "\nHeld By: " + PolicyHolder;
statement += "\n\nPolicy Summary\n";
statement += "Cost: \t" + totalAmount;
statement += "\nTax: \t" + tax;
statement += "\nTotal:\t" + grossTotal;

statement += "\n\nCars: ";
foreach (Insurable item in policy.Autos)
{
    statement += item.Name + "\n";
}
statement += "\nMotorcycles:";
foreach (Insurable item in policy.Motorcycles)
{
    statement += item.Name + "\n";
}
statement += "\nRVs:";
foreach (Insurable item in policy.RVs)
{
    statement += item.Name + "\n";
}
statement += "\nNumber of high risk drivers: " +
            risky;

return statement;
}
```

Listing 24 - Method to be Refactored

The supporting classes are shown next in Listing 25. These are obviously over simplified and their functionality (or lack thereof) really is not important for this discussion. These are necessary both to understand the code in Listing 24 and to see where some refactored code might end up.

```
public class BreakPointInsurancePolicy
{
    public String PolicyNumber { get; set; }
    public DateTime EffectiveDate { get; set; }
    public DateTime ExpiryDate { get; set; }
    public List<Person> People { get; set; }
    public List<Insurable> Autos { get; set; }
    public List<Insurable> Motorcycles { get; set; }
    public List<Insurable> RVs { get; set; }
}

public class Person
{
    public String FullName { get; set; }
    public int Age { get; set; }
    public int YearsDriving { get; set; }
    public int NumberTickets { get; set; }
    public int BasePremium { get; set; }
    public bool IsPolicyHolder { get; set; }
}

public enum InsurableType
{
    Automobile, MotorCycle, RV
}

public class Insurable
{
    public InsurableType VehicleType { get; set; }
    public double VehicleValue { get; set; }
    public String Name { get; set; }
    public static double RV_RATE = 0.005;
    public static double AUTO_RATE = 0.1;
    public static double MOTOR_RATE = 0.2;
}
```

Listing 25 - Supporting classes

The method in Listing 24 works. It builds and returns a summary statement for a given insurance policy. However it has a number of potential issues. They are:

- Unclear variable names
- Long method that does multiple things (calculates a type totals and builds a string)
- Repetitive code blocks
- Hard-coded values
- Some unnecessary temporary variables
- Excessive string concatenation

Refactorings will be applied in each case to address these issues and more. The code will be changed for better:

- Readability
- Testability
- Maintainability
- Logic
- Performance

To begin the discussion on refactoring the simplest thing is to use the immediate clues the IDE gives. Although it did not transfer to the code listing a certain part of the code is shown in the IDE with green squiggly lines beneath them. When hovering over a variable the popup shown in Figure 23 is shown. These would also show up as warnings when the code is compiled. The refactoring here is to simply remove them; that removes potential clutter and confusion.

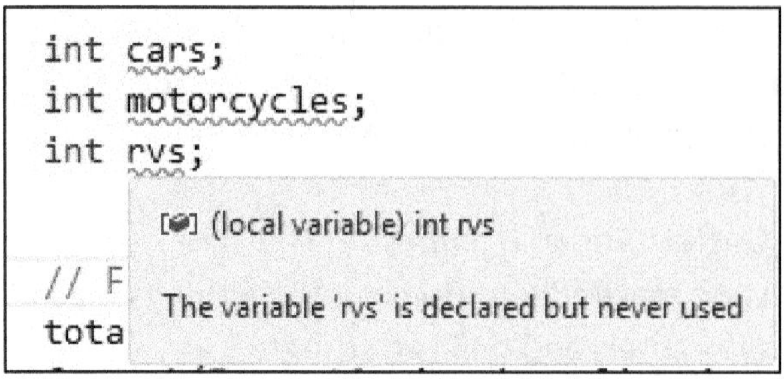

```
int cars;
int motorcycles;
int rvs;
        [♦] (local variable) int rvs
// F
        The variable 'rvs' is declared but never used
tota
```

Figure 23 - Unused Variables

Variables names should easily reveal their purpose. This helps with both maintenance and enhancement. For instance, what does "total1" really hold? From some analysis it can be inferred that it holds the total of the policy's automobile costs. The same with "total2" – the total of the motorcycle costs.

The refactoring commands in Visual Studio are accessible a number of different ways. They are also context driven, meaning that depending on what is selected when the commands are accessed, different command will be available.

The full set of refactoring commands is available from the Refactoring menu. This is available at Edit->Refactor and shown in Figure 24. Note that quick-key combinations are given for each command as well. If a command is chosen that does not make sense for what is selected an error dialog will be shown.

Refactor	▶	🔲	Rename...	F2
Next Method		🐑	Extract Method...	Ctrl+R, M
Previous Method		🔲	Encapsulate Field...	Ctrl+R, E
42	total2 = 0.0;	ℒₒ	Extract Interface...	Ctrl+R, I
43	foreach (Insu	🔳	Remove Parameters...	Ctrl+R, V
44	{	🔳	Reorder Parameters...	Ctrl+R, O

Figure 24 - Refactor Menu

In the case of the "total" variables, they should be renamed to be more descriptive. Different version of Visual Studio visually handle this differently. As of this writing Visual Studio 2015 creates a small pop-up option/summary window and highlights the variable to be renamed as shown in Figure 25.

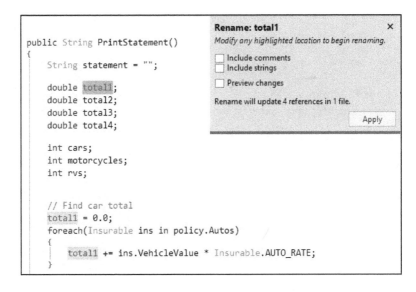

Figure 25 - Renaming a Variable

Directly typing in a highlighted instance will rename all the instances in the file. In this case the declaration was the instance selected and chosen for the Rename command but any usage may be chosen. The instances will be updated in real time as one types, but will not be finalized until the "Apply" button is clicked. If there are potential issues with the name such as a naming conflict (i.e. there was already a policyTotalCars somewhere else) this would be shown in the dialog box.

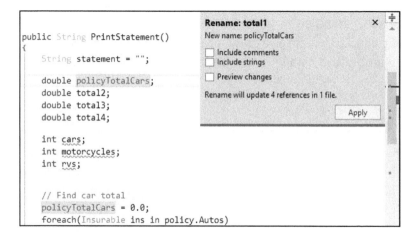

Figure 26 - Typing a new Variable name

A note about the "Preview Changes" – if this is chosen a dialog box will be shown after clicking "Apply" that will highlight each instance and allow the user to confirm/deny each instance. If not checked all instances will be changed immediately. Also in Figure 26 - the scroll bar area contains small dots to show where instances of the variable are located.

Next would be to remove the repetitive code. Notice how for each total a similar loop is used. In each loop the same property, `VehicleValue`, is multiplied by a respective factor and summed. This can pulled out and made into a general method.

The first step is to select the variable initialization and the `for` loop and choose "Extract Method" from the refactoring menu. Visual Studio will do its best to pull a method out that replicates the functionality, create that method at the end of the file, and allow the developer to rename the method. These two separate new code sections are shown in Figure 28 and 27 respectively. At this point "NewMethod" can be renamed to "FindTotalForCars" just like the variables earlier.

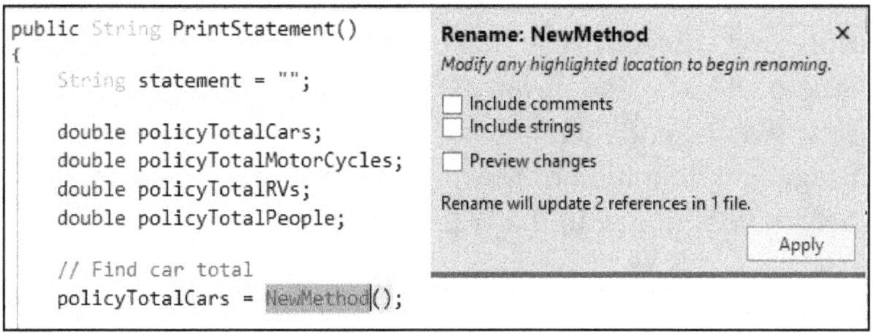

```
public String PrintStatement()
{
    String statement = "";

    double policyTotalCars;
    double policyTotalMotorCycles;
    double policyTotalRVs;
    double policyTotalPeople;

    // Find car total
    policyTotalCars = NewMethod();
}
```

Rename: NewMethod   ×

Modify any highlighted location to begin renaming.

☐ Include comments
☐ Include strings

☐ Preview changes

Rename will update 2 references in 1 file.

Apply

Figure 27 - Renaming a New Method

```
private double NewMethod()
{
    double policyTotalCars = 0.0;
    foreach (Insurable ins in policy.Autos)
    {
        policyTotalCars += ins.VehicleValue * Insurable.AUTO_RATE;
    }

    return policyTotalCars;
}
```

Figure 28 - Extracted Method

Each for loop could be extracted this way and a newly
named method would replace them. Although three new
methods would be introduced there are benefits as well.
The PrintStatement method is becoming cleaner and
new tests could be written to ensure proper total
calculations.

Note that carefully selecting the code is important. Visual
Studio will infer the new method signature and code from
this selected code but it is not always correct. Both the
usage and definition of the method must be inspected
before finalizing with the "Apply" button.

As an example of different methods being generated for a
different selection, consider what would happen if all three
loops were selected before choosing Extract Method. In this
case a "NewMethod" with out parameters is generated as
shown in Figures 29 and 30.

```
public String PrintStatement()
{
    String statement = "";

    double policyTotalCars;
    double policyTotalMotorCycles;
    double policyTotalRVs;
    double policyTotalPeople;

    // Find car total
    NewMethod(out policyTotalCars, out policyTotalMotorCycles, out policyTotalRVs);
```

Rename: NewMethod   ✕
Modify any highlighted location to begin renaming.

☐ Include comments
☐ Include strings
☐ Preview changes

Rename will update 2 references in 1 file.

Apply

Figure 29 - Result of Replacing All Loops

```
private void NewMethod(out double policyTotalCars,
                       out double policyTotalMotorCycles, out double policyTotalRVs)
{
    policyTotalCars = 0.0;
    foreach (Insurable ins in policy.Autos)
    {
        policyTotalCars += ins.VehicleValue * Insurable.AUTO_RATE;
    }

    // Find motorcycle total
    policyTotalMotorCycles = 0.0;
    foreach (Insurable ins in policy.Motorcycles)
    {
        policyTotalMotorCycles += ins.VehicleValue * Insurable.MOTOR_RATE;
    }

    // Find RV total
    policyTotalRVs = 0.0;
    foreach (Insurable ins in policy.RVs)
    {
        policyTotalRVs += ins.VehicleValue + Insurable.RV_RATE;
    }
}
```

Figure 30 - Method Replacing All Loops

While both "Extract Method" examples above work to clean up the code and create new methods, there is also a third procedure that is often used. This involves starting with a refactored method created by Visual Studio and then manually editing it and the code. This may be because Visual Studio does not quite do what is desired or because after automatic refactoring a better solution is found.

In the case of calculating the policy type totals the approach shown in Figures 27 and 28 is the starting point. The new method would be called `CalculateTypeTotals`. After renaming the method, an argument is added of type `InsurableType`. This value can then be used in the method to determine both the type and rate, loop using the appropriate values, and return the total. With this new method in place, along with a similar refactoring for the people total, the repetitive for loops in the original `PrintStatement` are now simplified to what is shown in Figure 31. The final `CalculateTypeTotals` is shown in Figure 32.

```
policyTotalCars = CalculateTypeTotals(InsurableType.Automobile);

policyTotalMotorCycles = CalculateTypeTotals(InsurableType.MotorCycle);

policyTotalRVs = CalculateTypeTotals(InsurableType.RV);

policyTotalPeople = FindPersonsTotal();
```

Figure 31 - Finding Type Totals

While this is certainly an improvement over the original method it can be refactored even further. Although it may be necessary at some point to store the individual totals, as the method stands now there is no use of these total variables other than to sum them for the policy total. So these variables could be totally removed and the method calls put in their place. The entire first part of the method in Listing 24 can this be condensed as shown in Figure 33.

```
private double CalculateTypeTotals(InsurableType it)
{
    double typeTotal = 0.0;
    List<Insurable> theList;
    double rate;

    if (it == InsurableType.Automobile)
    {
        theList = policy.Autos;
        rate = Insurable.AUTO_RATE;
    }
    else if (it == InsurableType.MotorCycle)
    {
        theList = policy.Motorcycles;
        rate = Insurable.MOTOR_RATE;
    }
    else if (it == InsurableType.RV)
    {
        theList = policy.RVs;
        rate = Insurable.RV_RATE;
    }
    else
    {
        return 0.0;
    }

    foreach (Insurable ins in theList)
    {
        typeTotal += ins.VehicleValue * rate;
    }

    return typeTotal;
}
```

Figure 32 - Refactord CalculateTypeTotals Method

The new method `CalculateTypeTotals` can easily have a unit test written for it. This is allows for finer-grain testing. Any future refactorings could also include tests and overall the system can be coded to be more stable. Those tests are not shown here.

```
String statement = "";

// Find policy total
Double totalAmount = CalculateTypeTotals(InsurableType.Automobile) +
                     CalculateTypeTotals(InsurableType.MotorCycle) +
                     CalculateTypeTotals(InsurableType.RV) +
                     FindPersonsTotal();

Double tax = totalAmount * 0.05;
```

Figure 33 - Condensed Total Calculation

The next change is to remove the hardcoded value for the tax rate, shown both in Listing 24 and Figure 33. Once again this could be a two-step automatic/manual process or a completely manual process. The automatic process using the refactoring menu is shown in the screen snippet of Figure 34. This would simply replace the hardcoded value with a class constant. This would be useful if the value was not expected to change. If this change is accepted the line in dark green is added at the top of the file and the lines below represent change (0.05 is changed to "V"). Once this is accepted a standard "Rename" process (Figures 25/26) is used to rename "V" to a more descriptive name.

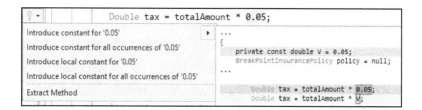

Figure 34 - Replacing a Value with a Constant

In the case of TAX_RATE (V was renamed to TAX_RATE) it is more beneficial to have this be a property rather than a constant. This would allow it to be set by the calling class. To further refactor this, a manual removal of the `const` attribute allows for using the refactor menu again. After selecting the TAX_RATE and choosing Encapsulate Field the dialog in Figure 35 is shown. This is used to preview how the field will be coded as a property with a getter and setter. After applying the changes a normal rename can be done to change the name from `TAX_RATE1` to a descriptive phrase such as `StatementTaxRate`. It has a default value of 0.05 as shown but can also be set by the calling code.

Two other refactors needed in Listing 24 deal with proper location of attributes. There are two similar loops, both of which look through all the people in the policy. One loop counts the number of risky people and the other examines each to see if they are the policy holder.

A first order refactoring would be to improve performance by handling both situations in one loop. This is shown in the screenshot of Figure 36. Two loops are replaced by one and both values are determined using the same `Person`. Performance is improved by looping through the `People` collection only once and not creating new `Person p` temporary objects in two different places.

However this still hides the actual problem – the `PrintStatement` method is tasked with determining details the policy should provide. Notice how `PolicyNumber` is exposed as a property; both the name of the policy holder and the number of risky people should be exposed by the policy in the same manner.

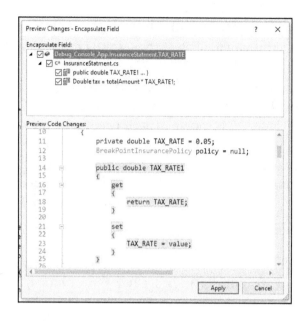

Figure 35 - Refactoring a Value to a Property

```
String PolicyHolder = "None Specified";
int risky = 0;
foreach (Person p in policy.People)
{
    if (p.Age < 25)
    {
        risky += 1;
    }
    if (p.IsPolicyHolder)
    {
        PolicyHolder = p.FullName;
    }
}
```

Figure 36 - Combining Loops

Changes to the `BreakPointInsurancePolicy` class to properly expose the number of risky drivers and the policy holder are shown in Figure 37. After these changes the statements in the `PrintStatement` are greatly simplified and shown in Figure 38.

```
public int NumberOfRiskyDrivers
{
    get
    {
        int risky = 0;
        foreach (Person p in this.People)
        {
            if (p.Age < 25)
            {
                risky += 1;
            }
        }
        return risky;
    }
}

public Person PolicyHolder
{
    get
    {
        return (People.Where(n => n.IsPolicyHolder == true).First());
    }
}
```

Figure 37 - Property Statements

```
String PolicyID = policy.PolicyNumber;
int risky = policy.NumberOfRiskyDrivers;
String PolicyHolder = policy.PolicyHolder.FullName;
```

Figure 38 - Updated PrintStatement

The final refactoring to be applied to the
`PrintStatement` method is another performance
enhancement. Repeated concatenation of `String`
variables is .NET (and many other modern languages) is very
expensive due to `Strings` being immutable. So once a
`String` is given a value it never changes. What appears to
be a concatenation with the += operator is in fact the
creation of a new `String` of the appropriate length
(determined by the arguments) and the copying of the
values into it.

The .Net framework has a class that is optimized for
dynamic string operations. The use of this class,
`StringBuilder`, and its `Append()` method to is much
more efficient than using `Strings`. When finished the
`StringBuilder.ToString()` method is used to
render the completely built string. The snippet shown
below is an example of using this class.

```
StringBuilder statement = new StringBuilder();
statement.Append("Insurance Policy: " + PolicyID);
statement.Append("\nHeld By: " + PolicyHolder);
statement.Append("\n\nPolicy Summary\n");
statement.Append("Cost: \t" + totalAmount);
statement.Append("\nTax: \t" + tax);
statement.Append("\nTotal:\t" + grossTotal);

return statement.ToString();
```

Figure 39 - Using a StringBuilder

Once these `StringBuilder` refactorings have be completed (and the repetitive `for` loops removed to their own method) the resulting `PrintStatement` is shown in Listing 26. The method to print the names via a `for` loop is shown in Listing 27. Much like the previous method the "Extract Method" command was used and then augmented by changing the signature manually.

```
public String PrintStatement()
{
    Double totalAmount =
    CalculateTypeTotals(InsurableType.Automobile) +
    CalculateTypeTotals(InsurableType.MotorCycle) +
    CalculateTypeTotals(InsurableType.RV) +
                    FindPersonsTotal();

    Double tax = totalAmount * StatementTaxRate;

    Double grossTotal = totalAmount + tax;

    String PolicyID = policy.PolicyNumber;
    int risky = policy.NumberOfRiskyDrivers;
    String PolicyHolder =
                    policy.PolicyHolder.FullName;

    StringBuilder statement = new StringBuilder();
    statement.Append("Policy #: " + PolicyID);
    statement.Append("\nHeld By: " + PolicyHolder);
    statement.Append("\n\nPolicy Summary\n");
    statement.Append("Cost: \t" + totalAmount);
    statement.Append("\nTax: \t" + tax);
    statement.Append("\nTotal:\t" + grossTotal);

    statement.Append("\n\nCars: ");
    PrintNames(statement, policy.Autos);

    statement.Append("\nMotorcycles:");
    PrintNames(statement, policy.Motorcycles);
```

```
statement.Append("\nRVs:");
PrintNames(statement,policy.RVs);

statement.Append(
    "\nNumber of high risk drivers: " + risky);

return statement.ToString();
}
```

Listing 26 - Refactored PrintStatement

```
private void PrintNames(StringBuilder statement,
                        List<Insurable> items)
{
    foreach (Insurable item in items)
    {
        statement.Append(item.Name + "\n");
    }
}
```

Listing 27 - Refactored PrintNames

Through the use of manual code changes and commands available in the IDE, a long method with several unclear statements was changed into a method that is shorter and easier to understand, maintain, and enhance if necessary. The variable names are clear and their meaning is evident. The bulk of the calculation work is done in separate methods that can be easily tested. Also, the method in Listing 27 could be refactored a bit further but this is left as an exercise for the reader.

From the list on [*Refactoring*] several were used, some several times and in combination with others:

- Encapsulate Field
- Extract Method
- Replace Temp with Chain
- Replace Magic Number with Symbolic Constant
- Add Parameter

Performance refactoring was also used. Combining statements into a single for loop is a common enhancement. Using a `StringBuilder` is another enhancement that can save resources and increase performance.

Refactoring Using Patterns

Design patterns are discussed thoroughly in another *Just Enough* book as well as several other resources. For that reason an in-depth explanation will not be given here. In regards to this final topic on refactoring only a brief explanation is needed.

Essentially design patterns are a standard way of arranging classes and components in a predetermined structure with a specific functionality desire. There are three broad categories: behavioral, structural, and creational. There are many standard patterns in each category and each describes arranging code in a certain way. Most are language agnostic and can be implemented in different languages.

Some patterns are so common that developers may use them and not be aware of it. In the code listings in previous sections the `foreach` statement was used; this is possible because the collection classes (`List` in the previous code) implement the *Iterator* pattern that allows for stepping through collection elements one at a time.

Another behavioral example is button events in GUI programming. Most of these are examples of the *Observer* pattern – a design that allows for publish/subscribe functionality. The GUI button "publishes" events when clicked, other classes may "subscribe" to receive the events and act on them accordingly.

A creation pattern is a way to create objects. One of the most easily understood is the *Singleton* pattern. In this pattern only a single instance of a particular object is allowed to be created.

Design patterns are generally coded into software from the start of development and their standard implementation allows for understandable statements in technical design documents. A design statement such as "Insurable objects will be dynamically created via an Insurable Factory" would let any implementer know how the code is to be written.

Design patterns can also be used in refactoring. As mentioned earlier one goal of refactoring is making code more maintainable. Design Patterns achieve that through arranging code in a way that can be referenced by name, thus any developer maintaining the code would know the structure and purpose of the code. When looking at was to refactor and restructure code Design Patterns can be very useful.

One of the simplest patterns is a creational pattern known as the Factory Method Pattern. This is a pattern that enforces an object to be created in a certain way; most often through a `static Create` method. In Listing 25 the `Insurable` class has no defined constructors meaning that a default no-argument constructor is available. As an example of refactoring using a pattern the code shown in Listing 28 is added to the class thereby enforcing all instances of `Insurable` be created in a known manner with the same method.

In the simple case of the current `Insurable` class this may seem like overkill. A normal public constructor would accomplish the same thing. However using the factory `Create` method, even in this simple example, accomplishes more than enforcing a way of creating Insurables.

A further refactoring of the `Insurable` class would be to remove the reliance on `InsurableType` and use the refactoring "Replace Type Code with Polymorphism" [*Refactoring*]. In this way the `Insurable` class becomes a base class and `Automobile`, `MotorCycle`, and `RV` become distinct derived classes. The `Create` method, located in the base class, can determine which derived class to return and perform any necessary initialization in one place rather than in each derived constructor.

A very good reference on combing Design Patterns and refactoring is listed in the bibliography (Kerievsky).

```
private Insurable() { }

public static Insurable Create(InsurableType iType,
                               String Name)
{
    Insurable ins = null;
    switch (iType)
    {
        case InsurableType.Automobile:
            ins = new Insurable()
            {
                Name = Name,
                VehicleType =
                    InsurableType.Automobile
            };
            break;
        case InsurableType.MotorCycle:
            // Creation code removed
            break;
        case InsurableType.RV:
            // Creation code removed
            break;
        default:
            ins = null;
            break;
    }
    return ins;
}
```

Listing 28 - Factory Method

Summary

This book demonstrates three software engineering concepts that are often grouped together – debugging, unit testing, and refactoring. Although the code examples are fairly simple the foundational concepts shown here can be extended to any size project.

While the techniques shown in the debugging section are very useful nothing is a substitute for actually debugging code. There are just too many ways for software to fail and many moments in debugging fall into the category of "I've seen that before and this is what fixed it." That is nearly impossible to replicate in a book. The mechanics of stepping through code, placing breakpoints, inspecting variables, and examining logs and stack traces were shown as those form the base of debugging intuition.

While this book only uses C# and Visual Studio, many of the same refactoring capabilities exist in other IDEs and languages. Eclipse, NetBeans, and X-Code all have similar capabilities for their respective languages. And as mentioned in Debugging and Unit Testing there are many similar logging frameworks available as well.

Bibliography

Apache Logging Project (website)
   http://logging.apache.org/

Fowler, M., et al. *Refactoring: Improving the Design of Existing Code* Reading, MA: Addison-Wesley

Jebaraj, Daniel (2013) *Unit Testing Succinctly*
   Morrisville, NC: SyncFusion

Kerievsky, J. (2004) *Refactoring to Patterns* Reading, MA: Addison-Wesley

Microsoft Developer Network (website)
   http://msdn.microsoft.com

NUnit Assertions (website)
   https://github.com/nunit/docs/wiki/Assertions

NUnit GitHub Wiki (website)
   https://github.com/nunit/docs/wiki/

Osherove, Roy (2013). *The Art of Unit Testing*
   Stamford, CT: Manning

Refactoring Catalog (website)
   https://refactoring.com/catalog/